Trapped in the Homeless Hustle

Trapped in the Homeless Hustle

ERICA MOSELEY

StoryTerrace

Text Cathy McIlvoy, on behalf of Story Terrace

Design Grade Design and Adeline Media, London

Copyright © Erica Moseley

First print August 2019

StoryTerrace

www.StoryTerrace.com

CONTENTS

PROLOGUE

My story will no doubt surprise and entertain you, but there's more to this book than that. The first part conveys to strangers as well as to those I've known along my journey the truth about my situation. I wanted my story written to help others know the truth, as I have often felt misunderstood. (I'm telling you my story not as a victim, but as a victor!) I want those of you I've met along the way to know that you've mattered in my life. My leaving abruptly had nothing to do with you. It was never easy to leave, but I had no control over it. If I've kept my distance, it's because I feared the pain I would feel having to leave you behind. After all, how many times can a heart be broken?

The second part of this book was written to inform everyone of the challenges and realities of homelessness. May you take to heart the plight of those living in a state of homelessness and help play a role in combating the problem. I have geared Part Two of this book to those who find themselves trapped in the "homeless hustle." My goal is to inspire and encourage you to emerge out of it successfully by offering you my tried-and-true homeless survivor tips. I've navigated homelessness for over twenty years—most of my life—so I can speak to your situation firsthand. It takes tenacity and skills to get through what you're experiencing and I'm here to help.

My own life's marathon continues and I'm running this race to win.

—Love, Erica

PART ONE

1

A BABY GIRL IS BORN
(*TENNESSEE, 1988*)

The American poet T.S. Elliot wrote, "Home is where one starts from." That's a nice sentiment and, for most folks living in America, I'm sure it's their reality. Yet my "start" (and well beyond) had little to do with "home." For most of my youth and on into adulthood, I either did not have a roof over my head or the roof I did have changed frequently, if not by the day. When we were briefly in a house or apartment, it wasn't ours. My father often said, "If your name is not on a lease, you're homeless." I was always very aware that our name was not on a lease. During those times when we were living under a roof, it was as guests and it was very temporary. It wasn't a home as most would define the word.

I started off life with two parents, but that scenario was short-lived. As they were both addicted to crack, chances are I was born a crack baby, though I can't say for sure. What I can say is that life, from the very beginning, was messy. Mom and Dad were Detroit-born and they were together for about thirteen years. At some point in their relationship they moved from Michigan to Tennessee and it was there they had me—their only child together. (I have three older half-siblings on my mother's side, but I've yet to meet them.) At the tender age of two, however, I lost my mother, not by death, which would have been tragic enough, but by willful abandonment. I believe this may be worse. I don't know what compelled her to do it, but one day she left us. She left me. So, you see, as Elliot's poem goes, the home I started from was transitory.

From then on, and for many years, life was lived one-on-one: Me and Dad. I was an innocent and fully dependent toddler when my homeless hustle began. And I learned from that moment forward that the term "home" would be an elusive one.

I also quickly learned the ins and outs of Greyhound Bus travel. When you don't have a place to call home, you'll likely find yourself searching for one, or at least on a journey of survival. Such was the case with me and Dad, and it was by Greyhound that we made our way across the United States and back again. We did this back-and-forth dance so many times and with so many stops in between (a.k.a. temporary starts), it makes my head spin just thinking about it. Life via the Greyhound shuffle was a whirlwind. Our frequency of travel and relocating also makes it a challenge for me to keep the timeline of my life clear. In the paragraphs and pages to follow, I'll do my best.

To add to our plight, a black man travelling alone with a young girl, even his own daughter, would often cause heads to turn. Curious onlookers would sometimes become suspicious (*Did he kidnap that little girl? Where's her mother? Why is he taking care of her? What happened?*) and Dad was questioned on more than one occasion. At other times, though, having me in tow probably helped us by making it easier for my father to get assistance for us in the form of vouchers for food at the bus stations, as well as other other types of help (more on this in the following chapters). My very first Greyhound adventure with Dad was in 1990. It was from Tennessee to Crenshaw, California. The journey took over two days. How my dad kept a young toddler from driving everyone crazy on such a long bus ride, I have no idea, but no one kicked us off and we eventually made it to our first of (too) many destinations together.

The new girl

2

ERICA EQUALS AMERICA
(*FIRST STOP: CALIFORNIA*)

A new girlfriend in Dad's life is more often than not what brought us to a different location, kept us there for a time, or sent us packing. The girlfriend factor and how it played out was a repetitive scenario that had me traveling across state lines time and time again, boarding Greyhound after Greyhound. In a very real way, girlfriends—more than just about any other factor—kept us on the move across America. Dad had a knack for meeting and wooing women and, as a result, a near constant stream of girlfriends came and went from our lives. This affected me, of course, because when each woman became part of my dad's life, she became, at some level, part of mine as well, whether I liked it or not.

Once we arrived in Crenshaw, a city in Los Angeles county, Dad met a woman and we moved in with her. (My grandfather lived in a nearby city at that time, but we didn't take up residence with him. He and Dad had a falling out or perhaps did not get along in general, I'm not sure which. Throughout my life, we were never taken in by relatives.) Being so young, I understandably came to believe that Dad's girlfriend at the time was my mother. After all, we lived together much like a normal family would. This girlfriend cared for me to some degree, we were settled in the house together, and I was even enrolled in school. But after her three-year relationship with my dad ended, I learned she was not my mother. This revelation cemented for me a mindset I continue to have to this day: I will never call anyone "Mom" again. This hurtful beginning made me extremely resistant to the many other girlfriends in my dad's life.

It was in Crenshaw I was first enrolled in elementary school and it would become the first of many classrooms where I would be deemed "the New Girl." Although I'm sure my teachers were given some background information on me, the other kids just knew what they saw: a little black girl wearing clothes from Goodwill. When others started the school year with new shoes, for example, I had on old ones from the thrift store.

Throughout my years in school, kids would soon question me and my situation, asking where I came from. I would lie and tell them whichever current girlfriend in my dad's life at the time was my mom and her children were my siblings. The other kids knew this didn't make sense (they had known my "brothers and sisters" and knew I wasn't a part of their families) and the questions would continue. Eventually what would come to light is that we were homeless. Such information would then be public and I was labeled "the Homeless New Girl." Bullying often followed. I decided early on that I would not take such abuse. It wasn't long before I learned to assert and defend myself by fighting with my peers in order to survive life at school. Miraculously, even in that often hostile environment, I also learned to take academics seriously, and I was a good student.

Enrolling me in school wherever we landed across America was a priority for my dad. He would drill into me these wise words: "You can be a productive citizen regardless of your situation." School was always first. It couldn't have been easy for him to secure my place in so many classrooms. We often came and went mid-year, sometimes several times during a given school year, but somehow he made it happen. He would enroll me with the address of a current girlfriend, or of a shelter, or a church. Dad wanted better for me. He didn't want me to be a stereotype and live homeless and uneducated. My school career began in California, but it would continue on in the many states where we lived throughout the years.

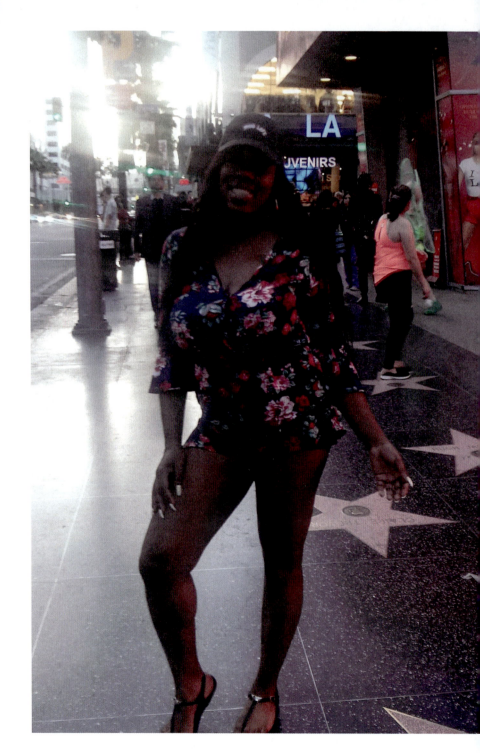

Erica in Hollywood

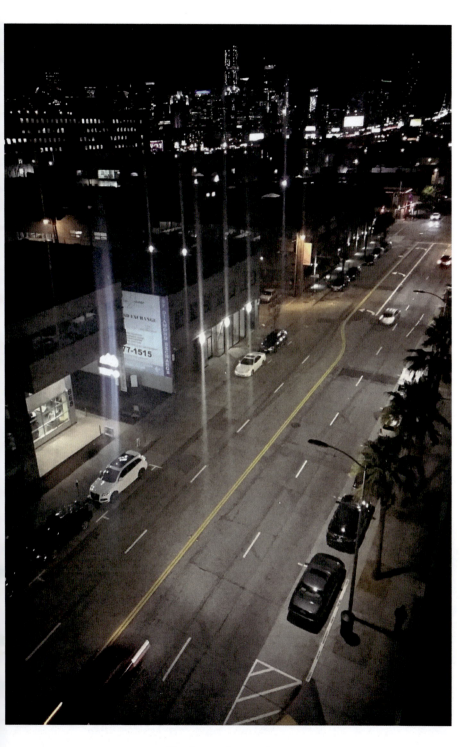

The views are better at the top

Dot my i's and cross my t's, all while homeless

Homeless I literally got it out the mud!

3

THE NEW YORK EXPERIENCE

was about nine years old when I boarded another Greyhound and travelled across the country from California to New York. I'm not sure what led us from west to east coast, but I'm sure it had something to do with breaking up with a girlfriend and/or drug problems. Thankfully, my dad was never incarcerated while I was in his care, but he continued to be addicted to drugs.

Once in New York, we found a place (or, more accurately, places) to stay through what was known then as the Emergency Assistance Unit (EAU). This system had us staying at a central location during the day and then we'd be bussed to a place to sleep for the night. Where we'd sleep changed each night. We were often put up in old buildings and even hospitals and then we'd return to the central location the next day to await our next "assignment" for the evening. The condition of the central location was deplorable—filthy, crowded, and the workers did not treat us well. Some nights the EAU did not come through and no place was provided for us to stay. For instance, if the only room available was in a domestic violence shelter, Dad and I would be out of luck. Only kids and moms were permitted to stay in those facilities—no men allowed—and Dad and I had to be kept together. So during these times, in New York and other places, we had no choice but to make our bed on the sidewalk. In these cases, Dad had a system to keep me safe. He would tie a shirt around me and himself so that if someone tried to move me, he would feel it and wake up.

During this transient time in New York, I attended several different elementary schools. Even after those nights of sleeping on the street, I'd be up in the morning, bussed back to the central location, and then I'd head off to school. After a long time, we were able to move into a two-bedroom apartment in the projects.

I'll never forget the view I had from that apartment—my bedroom overlooked the Empire State Building! For a while, my life seemed like it was becoming "normal." After school, I'd go to the Boys and Girls Club. Everyone knew me and I knew a lot of people. I had already gone to two or three different schools by that time, plus I knew people at the club, so I had lots of friends. I had proven myself and I fit in and was finally accepted. For the first time in my life, I was becoming popular. (When I first came to New York, in addition to being "the New Girl," I was also "the Cali Girl." I spoke like I was from California and the kids from New York picked up on my "accent" and the way I referred to everyone as "guys," as in "hey, you guys!") I became part of a group and it felt good. Attending so many schools required me to stay tough and prove myself over and over. This is a lot of pressure for anyone, but especially a kid and at times it took a toll, but I know those early experiences helped make me strong and become the woman I am today.

New York also brought with it some culture I enjoyed. I lived poor, but also rich as I was able to explore the city. I saw exciting landmarks like Times Square, and I ate a variety of good food that New York has to offer. But soon, it was time to hit the road again.

New York forever

The Bronx tale

4

ON THE ROAD AGAIN...
SEEING NEW PLACES AND MORE

As I mentioned earlier, I can not recollect the timeline of my life with 100-percent accuracy for the sheer fact that we moved so often. It is nearly impossible to keep all the moves straight, but what I do remember are the experiences and feelings I had even when I can't remember the exact year or age I was when each situation or incident took place. So, I continue on now as things unfolded in the days following our Brooklyn experience as best as I can...

Later, as we were living in New York, my grandfather called and told my dad he wanted to mend their relationship. He asked for us to come be with him in Las Vegas. He expressed to my dad that for my sake, he didn't want us living in Brooklyn in the projects. He had a house and we could join him there. So, Dad let go of our apartment, which we had received on assistance, and I was ripped away from my friends. Before I knew it, we were making our way to Nevada. It was a short-lived venture, however. Things, for whatever reason, did not work out between my grandfather and Dad, so we found ourselves homeless once again.

We went to Diffinax Springs, Florida, I believe, following our time in Nevada. I remember being on the hunt for my mom because her family lived there, but she was nowhere to be found. Perhaps she didn't want to be found by me and Dad. Still, as usual, I was enrolled in school, but this time after being in a classroom briefly, I was put back a grade. This had a profound effect on me. I was embarrassed that my former classmates saw that I had been put back—to the fourth grade when I should have joined them in the fifth. This is the moment that our homelessness really started to hit me. I remember thinking, *This is going to be my life so I'm going to have to work hard and keep my grades up.* I knew this wouldn't be my last school; I would be moving on at some point. I had to stay on top of things so I wouldn't continue to fall behind. I became more determined than ever and worked extra hard at school. Soon, I was allowed to go back to my actual grade level. From there, I became an A+ student in every state thereafter.

Following Diffiniax Springs, we went to Tallahassee and lived for a short time in an apartment. I clearly remember being in our apartment one night and hearing my dad experiencing an all-time low as he was heavy on drugs. I never saw my dad in the act of doing drugs, but I saw how his eyes looked after doing crack. I saw his body shake. On this night he was crying out for help. He told me God was telling him to get off drugs. I had witnessed him before, while under the influence of drugs, standing up and kneeling down over and over again, in a continuous motion. But now he remained in a kneeling position in the bathroom. He was in anguish. He was in a battle with addiction. It was a dramatic scene in our little apartment that day that is still etched in my mind.

It's around this time that Dad made me promise three things:

1) I'd finish school
2) I wouldn't get pregnant by age 16
3) I'd be a productive citizen

I kept these promises, though they were challenging, as we continued to be on the move.

At some point we lived in Houston, and an incident took place that I will never forget. I had finished doing homework at the library (the same library, I'm told, that Beyoncé, Kelly, and Michelle used to go to back in the day. I find that a fun coincidence so I just thought I'd share it with you). Anyway, my dad was supposed to pick me up after he got off work—he was working at a restaurant at that time—but I couldn't find him. This had become our routine after school. I'd go to the library and Dad would get me from there later in the afternoon. One fateful day, however, he was late and I panicked. Instead of staying put, I boarded a city bus to try and find him at his work. Eventually, I got off the bus (it was dark by this time) and I went to an apartment building and asked someone to help me. Thankfully, the man whose door I knocked on didn't harm me. He took me to the police station where I ended up being reunited with Dad. My father had called them earlier and reported me missing!

At that time, Children's Protective Services got involved when they learned we were homeless. Before we were housed in a shelter together, I was separated from my dad and put into foster care for a time. It was my first experience living the rich life. I was housed with a wealthy family. I lived in a five-bedroom house and I went to a privileged school. From there, however, I chose to reunite with my dad and we were housed in a shelter together. CPS kept an eye on me and Dad for a while to be sure I was being cared for properly.

And the bus rides continued...

New Orleans was "home" for a while. There we lived in a variety of places and spaces—a shelter, at the home of one of Dad's girlfriends, and at one point the homeless hustle had us living under a bridge. Like in New York, New Orleans brought with it some cultural experiences I'll never forget, like Mardi Gras and Louisiana cuisine.

Some time later, though, we boarded a bus back to California. This time, with a different girlfriend, we lived on Skid Row, an area of downtown Los Angeles that is known for its large homeless population. Many living on Skid Row are provided social services. Dad often chose the states and areas where he knew we would be more likely to obtain assistance. In Los Angeles, I continued as always, to attend school.

Our time on Skid Row wasn't long, of course, and before I knew it, we were back on a bus heading to New York. From New York, we returned to the west coast, only this time we went to the Pacific Northwest: Seattle. (By the way, I don't ever want to board another Greyhound again in my life. Do you blame me? You may be someone who loves being on a road trip, but these road trips were altogether too much. And they weren't for pleasure, but for survival.)

Once we reached Seattle, the homeless hustle

routine continued as normal: we stayed in a shelter and then moved in with another girlfriend. But something changed for me: I started my period. I bring this up because getting your period is a momentous event in a girl's life. Without a mother to inform me and help me understand the changes taking place with my body and emotions, it was an uneasy time. This is one incident I clearly recollect about Seattle, so it must have had a real impact on me.

I'm sure this also had to be a loud and clear signal to my dad that I was, indeed, growing up and becoming a woman. I remember sending him to the store to buy pads and he took forever to come back. Did he not know what I needed? I didn't feel I could ask my dad questions regarding puberty, nor could he relate to what I was going through as an adolescent female. I was a young teenager becoming a woman and I longed for that sense of wholeness that a nurturing mom provides, but I didn't have it. There were definitely different occasions growing up when I was hit by the reality that I only had a father. This was one of them.

There was something else I remember about Seattle: there were a lot of white people there, and Dad and I stood out. People wondered about this black man and young black girl living together. Questions swirled. We got stares. This wasn't New York or Los Angeles, where we could get a bit lost in the crowd.

Something I truly enjoyed about Seattle, though, was getting a taste of independence by earning a little money of my own. I became a bit of an entrepreneur and started my own side hustle. I'd go into the shelters and offer to do people's hair. I soon grew a reputation for being good at braids and popular styles and my clientele grew. People came to me so I could make them look and feel pretty. It was a good experience, but it wasn't to last. The girlfriend my dad had at the time announced that she had an apartment in South Carolina, so we were on the move again. The plan was that she would go there first and then we would soon follow and meet her. Once we arrived, we would all live in her place together. It didn't turn out that way, however.

Trap while homeless

It will get worse before it gets better

Cross your legs and keep your head up

I can see the future

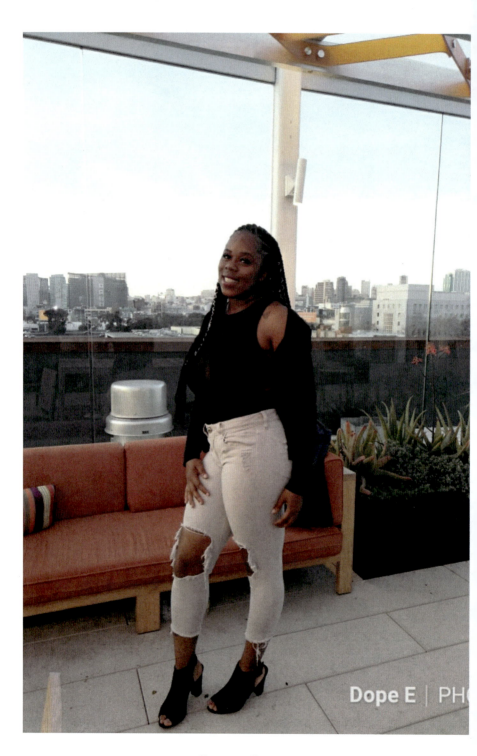

Forever standing strong

5

THE BACK-AND-FORTH SHUFFLE
(*SOUTH CAROLINA*)

We were given bus tickets to South Carolina (sometimes churches helped us out in this way) and arrived at the address we were given by Dad's Seattle girlfriend. We knocked on what we believed was her front door and waited around, but then realized we had been duped. Not only was she not there at the time, but, in fact, she didn't live there!

We were quickly faced with the reality that we didn't have a lot of choices in the state of South Carolina. For one thing, we had no other connections there. We were also now in the country and this area wasn't conducive to us sleeping on the streets. There were country homes nearby and there was the highway, but not much else. Where could we stay? Where could we get public assistance? No resources seemed to be available. In the midst of our predicament, provision was, once again, given to us.

The taxi driver who had taken me and Dad from the bus station to the apartment supposedly belonging to my dad's (ex)girlfriend, took pity on us. He graciously brought us to his house and let us stay there for a few days. True southern hospitality! During that time, my dad went back to the Greyhound station (I'm guessing to try and secure some tickets somehow) and, true to form, he met a woman who worked at the station. They ended up getting together and she took us in. We stayed with that girlfriend for about three years.

I went to school in South Carolina for middle school and the very beginning of high school, then we headed back to New York as the relationship between the Greyhound-Bus-Station girlfriend and my dad soured. I assumed that would be the last I'd see of her, but after a brief stint in the Bronx (my dad had begun filming documentaries on the subject of homelessness in New York at that time), I went back to live with this former girlfriend in South Carolina. Dad, then, made his way out west to spend time back at Skid Row, where he'd work on the second part of his documentary. And from there? We met in New York, again. New York to South Carolina, South Carolina to New York—back and forth. (Is your head spinning with all this to and fro? Mine was.) I was in the eleventh grade when I went back (again) to South Carolina.

It was then that a series of events took place that

would change things up for a while—new challenges, a new season to navigate. Children's Protective Services once again entered my life. I hadn't gotten lost this time and ended up at the police station. This situation was different. Dad and I had been arguing and my he whooped me that day. A woman heard what was happening and called CPS and they ended up taking me from him. As a result, from ages sixteen through eighteen, I was put in foster and group homes. I bounced back and forth. At times I felt as if I was being swung around like a rag doll.

Even during this tumultuous time I still managed to go to school, at least in some form. I attended alternative schools, which meant a few different scenarios; one scenario was that I went to school after the other students had been dismissed for the day. Then, myself and others who were in similar situations would be taught by a retired teacher or other staff member. I was afraid I might fall behind when I got back to regular school, but it all came together much better than I thought it would. It turned out that I had more than enough credits for my grade because New York schools required more units than the schools in South Carolina. Since I spent much of my secondary schooling in New York, I had earned enough credits. As a result, I was able to graduate from high school a year early, when I was seventeen.

Jesus take the wheel

Wheel of Fortune

6

GUESS WHAT? I'M PREGNANT.

Like setting up dominoes in a row and giving the first one a little push, events that took place as an older teenager in South Carolina set some new challenges in motion for me. Around this time, I met someone and our relationship would become intimate, changing my life forever. Through him, I would become a mother.

I met the father of my child while I was living in foster care. During our initial friendship, Luke (I have changed his name to protect his privacy) was the one who taught me how to navigate living in the south. I had lived in so many cities—Los Angeles, Brooklyn, the Bronx, New Orleans, Houston, Tallahassee and more, but living in southern country was a whole new ballgame for me! I was in every sense of the term a "city girl" and I felt comfortable in the hustle and bustle of urban living. In cities, I could easily get around on buses and I knew where to find resources to help me.

But here in South Carolina, life was different and, for me, challenging.

At age eighteen, I was released from the foster care system and Luke's grandmother took me in. Out of all the women I had lived with in the past, all of the girlfriends in my dad's life, it was Luke's grandmother who became like a mother to me. I still consider her like a mom to this day and I'm thankful for her. From the time I met her at around age sixteen, she taught me a lot about what means to be a woman. By nineteen, I was pregnant with her grandson's baby. This, as you can imagine, was a scary and devastating time for me. I wanted to have an abortion because even though Luke and his grandmother were in my life, I still questioned if they would truly be there to help me when I needed it. I agonized over how I would I get through this.

At this time my dad was living in California and I was still in South Carolina. I told him I was pregnant and he told me to come join him in California where more resources would be available to me and the baby. He had an apartment and I could live with him there, he said, so I boarded the all-too-familiar Greyhound and made my way to him. Unfortunately, it wasn't long before he lost the apartment and the two of us found ourselves together and homeless in L.A. once again, only this time I was with child. I'd been on Skid Row before, but never in this situation. To make matters worse, the father of my child stayed in South Carolina. Yet even in the midst of this chaos, I was determined to better myself and make a future. This drive seems to be something I was born with because it has always been a part of me. So, I took college classes and completed a course in computer office management.

As my belly continued to grow, Dad felt we should go up north to San Francisco and I should have my baby there. He felt the Bay Area offered more resources for families than Los Angeles. My daughter was born in a hospital in San Francisco. I delivered her alone—Dad stayed in the waiting room. I remained homeless until an apartment was provided for us in Oakland. I then went to school and earned a legal assistant certificate. From there, I attended Merritt College to become a paralegal and got a job at a law firm working for incarcerated women's rights. Part of my job required me to visit prisons and I was able to help these women. I'd tell them my story and what I'd been through because I wanted to encourage and inspire them. I liked the feeling of helping and serving others in this role.

It was a busy season, but once again I was provided the help I needed. I had a childcare provider at this time who was an angel! I could rely on this woman. She took care of my daughter during the day when I worked and at night when I attended school. She would even pick me up from school—a Godsend.

All in all, life was going along pretty well in Oakland. I was moving forward and I started to believe that maybe my life had been permanently changed. Perhaps I would never be homeless again. But those relaxed thoughts and feelings didn't last very long. Though Dad and I lived in that Oakland apartment for a while, it wasn't long before he decided to take off. I couldn't make rent by myself and I had no other family to help me. I felt I had no choice but to move back to South Carolina, baby in tow. It was an especially scary time for me. I kept thinking, *If I fall down, I'm really down—no safety net, no family and I am responsible for me and my daughter.* I felt the weight of that reality on my shoulders. I moved back in with Luke's grandmother.

After some time in South Carolina, I was offered a job, but it was in New Hampshire, so my daughter and I packed up and left South Carolina. I became a case manager at Verizon. New Hampshire, I soon discovered, was another "white" state, much like I found Seattle to be. At one point, I was discriminated against to such a serious degree that I went to court over it. Determined to win my case, I put in the hard work and did my research (I had learned a lot interning as a paralegal). All that effort paid off and I won my lawsuit!

I used the money I got from the lawsuit to make my way back to San Francisco, only this time I drove my own car instead of taking a Greyhound. A friend had invited me and my daughter to live with her in her apartment in the city. By this time, my little girl was seven years old. I thought San Francisco would be a better place for us to settle, so we moved in with my friend and I began to pursue an education in software development. I found and took advantage of free classes and programs offered. I was learning a lot and all was going well for about a month. Then, my girlfriend informed me that her boyfriend was getting out of jail and he would be moving back in with her. This meant my daughter and I had to leave her place. We were homeless once again.

"The more a daughter knows the details of her mother's life, the stronger the daughter." – Anita Diamant

A daughter is just a little girl who grows up to be your best friend

A mother's treasure is her daughter

7

DETERMINATION AND MY YOGA BUSINESS: THE MENTAL PAY OFF

Being trapped in the homeless hustle can either make you or break you. What I've learned over the years is that the key to not being broken in this game is determination and dedication. These qualities pay off. I've also learned that "no" doesn't mean no. "No" doesn't have to be solid or immoveable. It can often just mean "new opportunities." For me, it means "get up and do something different." You see, "no" can't be a no for me. I wouldn't survive if I accepted "no" for an answer. The word "no" has taught me to survive when I don't have anything because I won't let it stop me. "No" forces me to persevere.

After my friend told us we'd have to leave her apartment in San Francisco, my daughter and I lived out of my car. While my little girl attended school, I worked hard trying to find a job. I eventually landed a paid internship as a clerk for the City and County of

San Francisco. I was working for the city during the day, and living homeless in that same city at night. This seemed ironic. Our car was our bedroom, our closet, our shelter—it's all we had. My new job, however, opened doors as now I am certified to work for the city. As I'm sure you've seen from this brief story of my life, one thing can lead to another. (During this time, by the way, my daughter was on the honor roll at school. School in my life, and now in hers, remained a priority. To help distract her from our situation, I did what I could to give her time to play and be a kid. She even got to spend time at camp one weekend.)

Homeless with a child to care for—that makes the homeless war even more sobering. Besides looking for work, I also stayed busy doing everything I could to get us a place to live. I was put on every housing waiting list in the city, but I didn't just sit back and wait for them to call me. I kept pursuing. I ended up applying for and winning a housing lottery (I was chosen number 22 out of 10,000 people) and got a place for me and my daughter. The feeling of getting this apartment was euphoric! By the grace of God, miracles do happen, but more often than not you have to show up and put in the time and dedication to better your situation.

Another way I worked to get ahead was attending free classes offered at Code Tenderloin, networking with MV Code Club, Twitter, and other organizations and companies in order to try to secure work in sales or as a software developer. Having determination and dedication means staying busy in a variety of ways for the purpose of getting ahead and winning the homeless war.

Today, I'm also determined to be healthy emotionally despite all I've gone through living homeless most of my life. I'm determined to continue to learn and grow emotionally and spiritually. I'm learning how to be weak and express how I'm feeling. I'm learning to be sentimental. A constant challenge for me is to feel settled. Even in my current apartment, I hesitate to hang pictures on the walls. But, I want to be the best woman I can be for my daughter and to be an example for her of a healthy parent. I still have a lot of healing to do, but I'm moving in the right direction.

And I'm moving forward with my own business. I'm starting helloyogaqueen.com. I got this idea after taking yoga classes and realizing that my mental health is extremely important, especially while being homeless. Also, black women don't usually do yoga but they should! So, my idea is to sell yoga clothing and products that will appeal to women of all colors, shapes, and sizes. I want to encourage all women to do yoga, as it will help them become calm, lose weight, and help with mental health. As usual, I'm determined, and

I'm doing all I can to make this a successful business to help others along the way.

Queen—everyday fitness clothing designed for women of all color, shapes, and sizes

Hello Yoga Queen

PART TWO

8

HOMELESS SURVIVOR TIPS

Of course, I've had some help along the way in this crazy life journey I've been on, but what has been my most consistent, practical help throughout my life is putting to use the knowledge and skills I've acquired over the years. I've compiled many of these things in a list in order to share them with you here. I call them my "Homeless Survivor Tips" and they are valuable. I hope you'll give them some serious thought and take them to heart. Learn them. Put them to use. Share them with others. If you ever find yourself trapped in the homeless hustle, they will help you to survive it and even get out.

12 Homeless Survivor Tips (to keep in your back pocket):

1. Take care of your basic necessities for today. If you find yourself homeless, line up where you will sleep *tonight*. You need to eat *today*. You need to wash *today*. So find a shelter. Find a water source so you can get clean. Search out a public bathroom. Many folks on the street don't keep cleansing in mind, but it's important to look clean and not smell. Being clean will help open doors for you.

2. Don't get stuck. Here's where the mental game comes into play. Although you must take care of your basic necessities for today, you also have to think ahead. If you just stay in the moment, your situation won't change. Think of the future and move towards it. You do this by actively looking for opportunities. Go to the library and use their computer to do research. Computers are available to you for a set amount of minutes at a time. When your time is up, wait your turn and get back on the computer if you need to. Find public resources in your area that can help you and get busy seeking their services. Apply for jobs and cast your net wide. Start applying for public housing. When I was living in my car, I went to every housing non-profit organization that might help and told my story over and over again. As I mentioned in chapter seven, my dedication paid off.

3. Persevere. Your state of homelessness is not a one-day thing. You getting up and searching for opportunities is to be your ongoing routine, so do it every day. Get that in your mind and stick with the plan. Hang in there. Be strong. It'll pay off.

4. Get creative. Being homeless means you will need to put to use the abilities and skills you were born with or you've picked up along the way. You do have some, so use them. When you do, you can be a bit of an entrepreneur and better your situation. Remember how I used my skills doing hair to earn some money in Seattle? Selling drugs will get you in trouble and even land you in jail. That route is not creative, safe, or good. Instead, think of what you can do and find a way to make some money doing it. It may not be a lot, but every little bit helps.

5. Make connections. Meet others at various organizations, clubs, businesses, etc. Meet the right people and they can be a true asset. Before I won that housing lottery, a church put me up in a hotel for one month. By reaching out to them I made a connection and that connection was a real help.

6. Find what helps you be at peace. This is a stressful time for you and stress affects your body and mind in negative ways. You need a way to relieve some stress to survive this time. For me, it is yoga. When I discovered yoga, it made a huge difference in my life—it calms me. (It also became a business opportunity for me, as I mentioned earlier. Not every opportunity brings in money right away, but some do lead to financial gain.) For you, finding peace may be as simple as taking time to notice the beauty around you in a garden or at a park. Breathe.

7. Get an education. This tip not only helps bring about opportunities, but it will help distract your mind from your homeless situation and propel you forward. Distract yourself so you don't get depressed and lose the homeless war. Go to the Salvation Army, check out Eventbrite, visit the library and inquire about free classes or even fun things to do and learn in your city. Check out community services and see what they offer.

8. Limit your stuff. The more "stuff" you keep with you, the more you have to worry about. If you're living on the streets, where are you supposed to keep your things? The less you have, the easier you can get around. Be free of the burden of stuff and don't look homeless. You don't want to be hauling your crap around in a big trash bag or cart. This won't open doors for you. Lose the deadweight of any extra things you don't have to have.

9. Look presentable. I mentioned before the importance of getting clean and not looking homeless. You also need to dress for success. Go to the Salvation Army or Goodwill and get an outfit you can keep nice for job interviews. You don't need a full wardrobe at this point, just enough to look presentable and professional.

10. Save some money. Seriously. Saving doesn't just happen, you've got to make it happen, little by little. Money goes out quickly when you're living homeless, but try and save and invest. Invest in a hobby that could get you ahead and help you earn some money. Make sacrifices so you can save. Be strategic.

11. Don't put all your hope into people. Humans will let you down. Don't be naive and believe that everyone is there to help. They're not. You will receive some help along the way, no doubt, but you need to keep focus on your own dreams and goals and believe in your own abilities. Always have a plan B, as well as a plan C, D, E, and F— it is wiser than relying on people to open doors for you.

12. Don't let your past become the excuse for your present or your future. Unfortunate things happen, but, you can move forward if you don't blame your current situation on your past. Focus on this truth. Your current situation does not have to dictate who you are or will become. You will get through this. Your future can be better.

Yes, to some degree, unfortunate things happen to most people at some time in their life. And most don't know what to do if they lose their house, car, job, money, and/or mental stability. The tips about can help in a variety of situations, so remember them and put them to use as they fit your situation!

You can help others in a tough situation

There are also truths I'd like to share to those of you who are not trapped in the homeless hustle. Many in my situation are tempted to jump off the path of trying and even turn to drugs or other harmful things in hopes of escaping the pressure and pain of being homeless. Though many do go that route, I never did and not everyone does. Those living homeless need your encouragement. Don't write them off as hopeless. Many times, if given the opportunity for work, education, and housing, those living homeless can get out of their situation.

I hope to help end the stereotype of homelessness with this book. I want to be an example to others. Today I work at a non-profit organization helping homeless clients. I know it's my mission in life to play a part in resolving the homeless crisis. As I have had a wonderful case manager helping me at Hamilton Families, a non-profit organization in San Francisco, I'm determined to pay it forward and help others. One way I've been able to do this is by becoming a motivational speaker. I tell my story and speak on the subject of homelessness whenever I'm given the opportunity. This has become another way I can be an advocate for the homeless.

You can make a difference, too, and join me in kicking some homelessness butt! I challenge you to put yourself in a homeless person's place for a weekend and gain some understanding and empathy. Experience the street. Go to a shelter and talk with the people there. Listen to their story. Give some of your money, your time, your attention to an organization doing good work on behalf of homeless people. Also, buy some copies of this book and give it to your friends, family, and those in need of encouragement. Contact me and let's make a movie out of my story! There's so much we can do to offer practical help and raise awareness of the homeless crisis in America. Won't you join me?

Don't lose the homeless war!

Made in the USA
Columbia, SC
30 June 2023

19782818R00042